S0-BNA-730

THE QUOTABLE
CHURCHILL

A Prime Collection of Wit & Wisdom

RUNNING PRESS
PHILADELPHIA · LONDON

A Running Press Miniature Edition™
©1998 by Running Press
All rights reserved under the Pan-American and International
Copyright Conventions
Printed in China

British Library Cataloguing-in-Publication Data
A catalogue record for this book is available from the British Library.

ISBN-13: 978-0-7624-0240-3
ISBN-10: 0-7624-0240-7

This book may be ordered by mail from the publisher.
Please include £1.00 for postage and handling.
But try your bookstore first!

Running Press Book Publishers
Cedar House
35 Chichele Road
Oxted, Surrey RH8 0AE

Contents

Introduction

Sir Winston Churchill's words defined the political landscape of an era—and forever changed the course of human history. The eloquence and passion of his wartime speeches galvanised the British nation in its heroic stand against the Nazi aggression that had brought the Continent to its knees, and rallied peoples from all corners of the earth to join in the fight for freedom. After the conflict's end, he was the first to fully comprehend the new dynamics of the Cold War world—he coined the term 'Iron Curtain', dedicated himself to trans-Atlantic co-operation, and called for a 'United States of Europe'.

During his long public career, Churchill served six

monarchs, fought in battles on four continents, and served 62 years in Parliament, holding Cabinet offices such as Undersecretary of State for the Colonies, Home Secretary, and First Lord of the Admiralty, in addition to his two terms as Prime Minister. Further, Churchill wrote 42 volumes of history, memoir, essays, and collected works, a myriad of journalistic articles and countless speeches, for which he never employed a speechwriter. For his service to the crown and to the world, he was named a Knight of the Garter; for his service to the world of letters, he was awarded the Nobel Prize for Literature.

To merely list Churchill's tremendous achievements, however, would not fully illuminate the breadth of his experiences and interests. As well as soldier, statesman, and orator, he was a talented painter, a successful sportsman, and a unionised stonemason. He was not only a great writer, but moreover a great wit: 'In my behalf,' he once said, 'you cannot deal with the most serious things in the world unless you can understand the most amusing'. For this reason, the editors have included an ample array of Sir Winston's wisdom, ridiculous and sublime, in the pages that follow, so that all may enjoy the heart, humour, and humanity of the man who changed the world.

CHURCHILL
ON LIFE

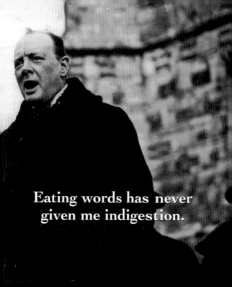

Eating words has never given me indigestion.

By being so long in the lowest form [at Harrow School] I gained an immense advantage over the cleverer boys. They all went on to learn Latin and Greek and splendid things like that. But I was taught English. . . . Thus I got into my bones the essential structure of the British sentence—which is a noble thing.

Headmasters have powers at their disposal with which Prime Ministers have never yet been invested.

Personally
I am always
willing to learn,
although I do
not always like
being taught.

A fanatic is
one who can't
change his
mind and
won't change
the subject.

It is a fine thing to be honest, but it is also very important to be right.

It is better to be making the news
than taking it, to be an actor rather
than a critic.

An appeaser is one who feeds
a crocodile—hoping it will
eat him last.

Don't argue
about the
difficulties.
The difficulties
will argue
for themselves.

Note to an editor scolding him not to end a sentence with a preposition:

This is the sort of impertinence up with which I will not put.

To Arab leader Ibn Saud, upon being told the king's religious beliefs forbade the use of tobacco and liquor:

I must point out that my rule of life prescribes as an absolutely sacred rite smoking cigars and also the drinking of alcohol before, after, and if need be during all meals and in the intervals between them.

When I was younger I made it a rule never to take strong drink before lunch. It is now my rule never to do so before breakfast.

All I can say
is that I have
taken more out
of alcohol than
alcohol has taken
out of me.

Lady Nancy Astor:

Winston, if you were my husband, I'd put arsenic in your morning coffee.

Churchill:

Madam, if you were my wife, I'd drink it.

Bessie Braddock:
Winston, you are drunk!

Churchill:
And Madam, you are ugly.
And tomorrow, I'll be sober,
and you will still be ugly.

I t is hard, if not impossible, to snub
a beautiful woman — they remain
beautiful and the rebuke recoils.

The price
of greatness
is responsibility.

Courage is rightly esteemed the first of human qualities . . . because it is the quality that guarantees all others.

CHURCHILL
AT WAR

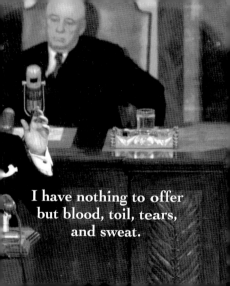

I have nothing to offer
but blood, toil, tears,
and sweat.

To Prime Minister Neville Chamberlain, following the Munich agreement:

You were given a choice between war and dishonor. You have chosen dishonor and you will have war.

Y ou ask, what is our policy? I
will say: it is to wage war, by
sea, land, and air, with all our
might. . . . You ask, what is our aim?
I can answer in one word: victory.
. . . Victory at all costs, victory in spite
of all terror, victory however long and
hard the road may be; for without
victory there is no survival!

—*First statement as Prime Minister*

We shall not flag or fail. We shall go on to the end, we shall fight in France, we shall fight on the seas and oceans, we shall fight with growing confidence and growing strength in the air, we shall defend our Island whatever the cost, we shall fight on the landing grounds, we shall fight in the fields and in the streets, we shall fight in the hills; we shall never surrender.

—*Speech following the Dunkirk evacuation*

Let us therefore brace ourselves to our duties, and so bear ourselves that if the British Empire and its Commonwealth last for a thousand years, men will still say: 'This was their finest hour'.

—*Speech before the Battle of Britain*

Never in the field of human conflict was so much owed by so many to so few.

—*Tribute to the Royal Air Force following the Battle of Britain*

Death and sorrow will be the companions of our journey; hardship our garment; constancy and valor our only shield. We must be united, we must be undaunted, we must be inflexible.

[In war] the
latest refinements
of science are linked
with the cruelties
of the Stone Age.

On the parachute landing of Rudolf Hess in Scotland:

This is one of those cases in which the imagination is baffled by the facts.

On the Nazi invasion of the Soviet Union:

f Hitler invaded Hell I would make at least a favourable reference to the Devil in the House of Commons.

To Adolf Hitler:

We will have no
truce or parley with
you, or the grisly gang
who do your wicked will.
You do your worst—and
we will do our best.

The V sign is the symbol of the unconquerable will of the occupied territories, and a portent of the fate awaiting the Nazi tyranny.

Do not let us speak of darker days; let us speak rather of sterner days. These are not dark days: these are great days—the greatest days our country has ever lived; and we must thank God that we have been allowed, each of us according to our stations, to play a part in making these days memorable in the history of our race.

When I was called
upon to be Prime Minister,
now nearly two years ago,
there were not many
applicants for the job.
Since then perhaps the
market has improved.

On the victory at El Alamein:

This is not the end.
It is not even the beginning
of the end. But it is,
perhaps, the end
of the beginning.

In wartime, truth is so precious that she should always be attended by a bodyguard of lies.

'Not in vain' may be the pride of those who survived and the epitaph of those who fell.

The nation had the lion's heart.
I had the luck to give the roar.

Churchill
On The World

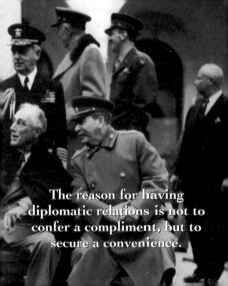

The reason for having
diplomatic relations is not to
confer a compliment, but to
secure a convenience.

On the office of Prime Minister:

If he trips he must be sustained; if he makes mistakes they must be covered; if he sleeps he must not be wantonly disturbed; if he is no good he must be poleaxed.

I do not resent
criticism, even when,
for the sake of
emphasis, it parts for
the time with reality.

On declining knighthood following the Tory defeat at the polls:

I could not receive the Order of the Garter from my sovereign when I received the order of the boot from his people.

61

Political ability: It is the ability to foretell what is going to happen tomorrow, next week, next month and next year. And to have the ability afterward to explain why it didn't happen.

On the Soviet Union:

I cannot forecast to you the action of Russia. It is a riddle wrapped in a mystery inside an enigma.

I always avoid prophesying beforehand, because it is much better policy to prophesy after the event has already taken place.

The English
never draw a
line without
blurring it.

The Almighty in His infinite
wisdom did not see fit to create
Frenchmen in the image of
Englishmen.

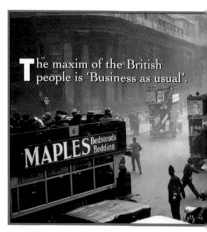

The maxim of the British people is 'Business as usual'.

The practice of Parliament must be judged by quality, not quantity. You cannot judge the passing of laws by Parliament as you would judge the output of an efficient Chicago bacon factory.

Democracy is
the worst system
devised by wit
of man, except
for all the others.

Dictators ride to and fro upon tigers which they dare not dismount. And the tigers are getting hungry.

Some Socialists see private enterprise as a tiger—a predatory target to be shot. Others see it as an old cow to be milked. But we Conservatives see it as the sturdy horse that pulls along our economy.

The inherent vice
of capitalism is
the unequal sharing
of blessings; the
inherent virtue of
socialism is the equal
sharing of miseries.

It is the socialist
idea that making
profits is a vice;
I consider the real
vice is making losses.

On Socialism:

Government of the duds, by the duds and for the duds.

CHURCHILL AND HIS CONTEMPORARIES

On Elizabeth II:

Lovely, inspiring. All the film people in the world if they had scoured the globe could not have found anyone so suited to the part.

**On Prime Minister James
Ramsey MacDonald:**

We know that he has,
more than any other man,
the gift of compressing
the largest number of
words into the smallest
amount of thought

On the administration of
Prime Minister Stanley Baldwin:

Decided only to be undecided,
resolved to be irresolute,
adamant for drift, solid for fluidity,
all-powerful to be impotent.

On Vladimir Lenin:

His sympathies cold and wide as the Arctic Ocean; his hatreds tight as the hangman's noose. His purpose to save the world: his method to blow it up.

On Prime Minister Neville Chamberlain:

He looked at foreign affairs through the wrong end of a municipal drainpipe.

On Sir Richard Stafford Cripps:

There, but for the
grace of God, goes God.

**On Sir Richard
Stafford Cripps:**

He has all of
the virtues I dislike
and none of the
vices I admire.

None of his colleagues can compare with him in that acuteness of energy of mind with which he devotes himself to so many topics injurious to the strength and welfare of the State.

On Edward F. Wood, Earl of Halifax:

Halifax's virtues have done more harm in the world than the vices of hundreds of other people.

**On General Bernard
'Monty' Montgomery,
Allied Commander:**

ndomitable in retreat; invincible in
advance; insufferable in victory.

On Charles de Gaulle:

Of all the crosses
I have to bear, the
heaviest is the
Cross of Lorraine.

On Charles de Gaulle:

England's grievous offence in de Gaulle's eyes is that she has helped France. He cannot bear to think that she needed help. He will not relax his vigilance in guarding her honour for a single instant.

On Prime Minister Clement Attlee:

He is a sheep in sheep's clothing.

Mr. Attlee is a very
modest man. But then he has
much to be modest about.

On Minister of Health
Aneurin Bevan:

I can think of no better step to
signalise the inauguration of the
National Health Service than that a
person who so obviously needs
psychiatric attention should be among
the first of its patients.

On John Foster Dulles,
U.S. Secretary of State:

He is the only case
I know of a bull who
carries around his own
china shop with him.

Eulogy for
Franklin D. Roosevelt:

He died in harness, and we may well say in battle harness, like his soldiers, sailors, and airmen who died side by side with ours in carrying out their tasks to the end all over the world. What an enviable death was his.

CHURCHILL
AT LAST

The greatest lesson in life
is to know that even fools
are right sometimes.

Politics are almost as exciting as war, and quite as dangerous. In war you can only be killed once, but in politics many times.

Definition of a politician:

He is asked to
stand, he wants
to sit, he is
expected to lie.

An optimist
sees an opportunity
in every calamity;
a pessimist sees
a calamity in
every opportunity.

I am an optimist. It does not seem too much use being anything else.

True genius resides in the capacity for the evaluation of uncertain, hazardous, and conflicting information.

Short words are best and the old words when short are best of all.

Personally, I like
short words and
vulgar fractions.

No one can
guarantee success
in war, but only
deserve it.

Never give in, never give in,
never, never, never, never—
in nothing, great or small, large or
petty—never give in except to
convictions of honour and good sense.

**On the rebuilding of the
House of Commons:**

We shape our buildings;
thereafter they shape us.

One ought to be just
before one is generous.

Men occasionally stumble over
the truth, but most of them
pick themselves up and hurry off as
if nothing had happened.

Writing a book is an adventure. To begin with, it is a toy and an amusement. Then it becomes a mistress, then it becomes a master, then it becomes a tyrant. The last phase is that just as you are about to be reconciled to your servitude, you kill the monster, and fling him to the public.

Out of intense complexities
intense simplicities emerge.

For my part, I consider that it will be found much better by all parties to leave the past to history, especially as I propose to write that history myself.

C H U R C H I L L

If the human race wishes to have a prolonged and indefinite period of material prosperity, they have only got to behave in a peaceful and helpful way toward one another, and science will do for them all they wish and more than they can dream.

120

We are happier in
many ways when we
are old than when we
were young. The young
sow wild oats, the
old grow sage.

When I look back on all these worries I remember the story of the old man who said on his deathbed that he had had a lot of trouble in his life, most of which never happened.

The farther
backward you can
look, the farther
forward you are
likely to see.

In War: *Resolution.*
In Defeat: *Defiance.*
In Victory: *Magnanimity.*
In Peace: *Good Will.*

Winston Churchill, his daughter and wife.

Photography Credits

This book has been bound using
handcraft methods, and is
Smyth-sewn to ensure durability.

The cover and interior were
designed by Toni Renée Leslie.

The text was edited
by Brendan J. Cahill.

Photo research was executed
by Susan Oyama.

The text was set in
Cochin and Futura.